52 Weeks of Grace

Edition One

52 Weeks of Grace

M.E. Lyons

authorHOUSE®

AuthorHouse™
1663 Liberty Drive
Bloomington, IN 47403
www.authorhouse.com
Phone: 1-800-839-8640

Published by AuthorHouse   02/21/2013

ISBN: 978-1-4817-1706-9 (sc)
ISBN: 978-1-4817-1705-2 (e)

Library of Congress Control Number: 2013903180

Contents

Dedication

This devotional guide is dedicated to all of those individuals who struggle from day to day to stay on the straight and narrow path, and are not ashamed to admit that living for Christ is a constant fight.

This devotional guide is also dedicated to a couple of members of our Church who often call me, text me and share with me word of encouragement when we feel a little challenged in the spiritual realm. I thank God for members who are not afraid to stand up for what is right and say, "Pastor be encouraged" and by the same token they are not too distant to say, "Pastor I believe this would be an advantageous approach to the present situation." I would call and list your names but you know who you are!

I would like to further dedicate this devotional guide to a diligent and committed aide in the Church I now Shepherd: Sister Annette Gray; she helps and always goes the extra mile when asked. Thank you for being so committed not to me, but to the cause of Christ.

I would be remised if I were not to ever make mention of a very special young man in the life of the Lyons'. Brother Frederic Stanley Tims, he is the Minister of Music at Goodwill, and by far he is perhaps the most committed, faithful and easiest to get along with musician I have ever worked with and have had the privilege of leading and we pray that God would bless you according to your deeds sir!

To a very close Christian couple: Pastor and Mrs. Marquise and Destiny Collins; whom we share in what we have come to find out is a close bond and friendship.

To my third grade teacher: Miss Dianne Chuha-Canon who was a very influential person who had a great deal of molding me into the person I am today!

Preface

In this devotional guide you will soon discover that the scriptures and applicable suggestions will aide and assist you in your weekly walk with Christ. Often there are many instances in life that cause us to stumble, and it will only be by the grace of God we are placed back on the straight and narrow. Grace is a subject that has become less talked about and we need it in the times we live even more evidently. If your life is anything like my life; and I am sure it is you would agree that scriptures help to direct, encourage and strengthen us in the trying times that lie between Sunday and Saturday. The busiest time of the enemy is after Sunday worship and before Bible Study; simply because if he can hinder us after a Word from God and before a Word of God, the seed has been withheld. In this devotional guide, we will delve into a few inspirationally given verses that will shun the enemy from planting any ill-gotten seeds into our minds and cause the great divide between us and God!

Introduction

My favorite scripture; and when we say favorite the scripture that ministers to me the most upon a daily basis would be Romans 8: 38-39. As a matter of fact before I preach any sermon this is our recitation! We use Paul's pronouncement as a precursor to our preachments for the last thirty one plus years in the ministry. God called us to the Gospel ministry at the tender age of four and we have been a believer that God places certain deposits in us for certain situations; and this deposit of Romans 8: 38-39 has been for a lifetime! In this devotional guide prayerfully, you will read scriptures and hear stories and exegetical highlights that would minister to you and ultimately lighten the load of your week, grant opportunities to become closer with our Lord and Saviour. If you allow this guide to speak to you not only on a weekly basis but every day of your life; it will enhance your walk with Christ; if you allow it to do so. Sit back, relax and take in week one and begin to see yourself in each scripture and expect a change for the better in your life!

APPLICATION ONE

Which Way Are You Headed?

Proverbs 16:17

As we begin this day; King Solomon the wisest man to have ever lived speaks somewhat of a riddle. He says: your way of traverse will divert you from evil; what does he mean? Does he imply that the direction I am headed will bring about terrible circumstances land me in a turbulent storm cause me to end in desolate measures? No, actually Solomon teaches us that whatever direction we are headed will determine what we will find at the end of the road. If you are saved then your direction should be pointed toward Heaven and heavenly places and people it actually suggests that the upright will shun from evil. In other words, when people around me begin to gossip, lie, and head in a direction we are not going; we depart from evil; which literally means; **RUN** in the opposite direction. Then Solomon says: it keeps my way and even preserves my soul and we all know the soul is the seat of our souls; which means if I stay on the path I won't be so disturbed, frustrated, annoyed because just as the R&B Artists Roberta Flack/Donny Hathaway says: "The closer I get to you"; and so it is with God, the closer we get to Him the better off we will be. Ask yourself the question:

When it comes to being at work, home, in the neighborhood or anywhere and evil is taking place: how can we get close to someone we have been running from?

APPLICATION TWO

No Excuses

John 5:6

John, the friend of Jesus, begins the story of another display of the power of God; speaks about a man that was lame, hurt, disabled, frustrated and seemingly upset for thirty eight long years. When we begin to read this portion of the story we would see this place was in the Hebrew tongue called Bethesda had a pool. This pool was said to at certain times have an angel descend upon it and trouble the waters and whoever stepped **INTO** the pool was healed of all of their infirmities. Check this out; there is a major difference in stepping **INTO** and staying **OUT OF**. The word troubled in this text means, to agitate. Some of us will experience some things this week that will agitate us; it might be your supervisor that continuously pushes our buttons, a child that won't do right, perhaps spousal issues, or maybe even family drama. Could it be financial frustrations? Whatever you do, don't make any excuses; the key is to learn how to step into what is agitated! I know, it doesn't make sense; well here it is; when we step into what is agitated we actually step out on Faith; remember Peter, he stepped out of what was solid to step into what was shaky, the water was agitated, that is why Jesus told the

AgItAtInG wAtEr: be still. So when things become agitated around us; don't complain; step in; because after you step in you will be able to step up: the man was able to walk afterwards! So the question we must ask ourselves is: "Do you want to be made whole?"

APPLICATION THREE

The Decision Is Yours!

Psalm 6:6

Transparency is a good thing! All of us at one time or another, awaken on the proverbial wrong side of the bed, have a knock down; drag out with our spouse, part ways with the best of friends, or has become spiteful towards a person who has wronged us. But in the scripture today David suggests that how you feel should be voiced to God, in order that He might help us. God will only aid those who are honest with Him about their true feelings. You see when we harbor hatred, anger, malice and even dislike towards others or things it can turn into inward depression and inward depression will ultimately become outward bitterness. David says, "I am tired of being tired and sick of being sick" I spend my nights in my bed swimming in my tears. I act like I am happy but sadness tends to always lay down with me. I even sit down on my couch and the valve of my tears runs freely; nothing seems to bring about relief. The shepherd suggests that if we are going to cry we at least need to know who to cry to. When you feel as if the walls are closing in on you, family is breaking up, or your job is too stressful, **instead of crying about it; CRY TO HIM**! He is always up. His ultimate goal is to give you rest in your bed and relaxation on your couch; CRY TO not about!

APPLICATION FOUR

A Little Deeper

Luke 5:5, 6

This week's scripture speaks about Jesus spending time with some fishermen and teaching them a very important yet encouraging lesson. He first teaches us that He knows much better than we what will work better to our own advantage. These fishermen were masters at what they did; but even at their masterful expertise they were vastly inadequate. Jesus speaks to Peter and the boys and says, "Go out into the waters and let your nets down." There are a few things we overlook about this scripture that we need remember. First thing He says is, "go out further than where your comfort level is" and then He says, "Let your nets down for a draught." I imagine you may say how does this speak to my life; glad you asked, we all have something that we are good at; but the fact is that no matter how good we are; Jesus still speaks and expects for us to go out a little further because there is always more fish to catch and deeper waters to explore. The trouble we have is we spend time in shallow waters expecting deep catches, we expect better families; but are not willing to invest proper time to make better families; stronger marriages; but will not take the time to get to know our spouses; higher paying jobs; but will not become a better steward with the one we have now! Deeper waters produce not only bigger catches but it also produces net-breaking happenings in our lives! Why not listen to the WORD that has gone forth this day, and launch out into the deep and expect **NET-BREAKING** catches, when this happens <u>YOU WONT HAVE ROOM ENOUGH TO RECEIVE IT</u>, but it all begins when you decide to move from where you are; to where you need to be into **<u>DEEPER WATERS</u>** They were so Blessed they needed help from their friends who were **WATCHING** them be Blessed! Tell someone you love today or send a text, set a reminder saying: **<u>I'M MOVING INTO DEEPER WATERS!</u>**

APPLICATION FIVE

Wait Your Turn

Proverbs 20:21

Wait your turn. Every day we deal with the hustle and bustle of life. Rushing trying to get certain places at certain times; we even are in a hurry to gain different things in life. Not to mention how anxious we are to obtain certain achievements in life by a certain time. We want to have the car we see our neighbor drive. Our good friends have married a good woman, or spouse and we endeavor to find someone that provides and cares the way they do as we sit back and watch. We are seemingly forced to look on when those we know are not living as spiritual as we are and here they are being blessed time and time again. I have but one thing to share with you on this Monday morning; **WAIT YOUR TURN!** Solomon has been named the wisest man that has ever lived outside of Christ and he shares a snippet and suggestion to us that appears to be prevalent for this day and age. He simply states: "An inheritance may be gotten hastily" which in our language of today reads: possessions may come quickly for some at first; but in the end it looks like a blessing but it's not. You see what seems to be a blessing for those who seemingly have it all; really is not because as Mama'nem used to say:

anything worth having is worth **working** and **waiting** on. I want to impress this thought into your minds; you know on every vehicle there are two side view mirrors and inscribed in the bottom of the mirrors are these words: Objects in mirror are closer than they appear; only to serve as a suggestion and reminder to each of us; although it seems afar off, its closer thank you think. Just wait your turn! So in essence Solomon would like to leave all of us with the thought that if it's easy, quick and simple it may be that it's not your turn. The way God works is we receive after we conceive! <u>CRAZY ISN'T IT</u>? We will not receive blessings until we bear burdens. Solomon once again says: if it is easy chances are that it is not a blessing who gives blessings? <u>GOD</u>. If God gives blessings; then the only thing we should do is: **WAIT YOUR TURN**! Make sure you share this wisdom with someone else by confirming that you will **WAIT YOUR TURN**!

APPLICATION SIX

Can You Handle The Truth?

Proverbs 12:17, 18

Isn't it funny how people may ask you a question and follow it by saying: and tell me the truth? Or a situation that as arose and you know the truth but will not offer it. This scripture today teaches us that regardless of their reaction or feelings; the truth is needed and in a real sense; almost demanded of us who know the truth but will not speak the truth! Once again we have been instructed to stop by and speak with that wise old man Solomon again, and he yields a word this morning that captures the attention of all of us; **SPEAK THE TRUTH**. Wow, truth sometimes is almost like an instance that we give when the recipient can handle it rather than when they need it. Consider how the scripture says, "but a false witness is like deceit" and deceit here means to betray. Sometimes, we feel like it is not our duty to tell some people the truth but what happens when we do not tell them the truth is like we are betraying them. Do you know why? Because **YOU ARE HIDING WHAT THEY NEED**. It's like someone being sneaky because now you almost have to hide things from them in order to **KEEP** the truth from them. But then on the contrary; the truth is unto righteousness; this word means:

it's like it builds up equity and when you have equity in a thing you can draw from it. Notice this: three things happen when we tell the truth. First off, the truth **HURTS**. There are many that do not want to know, simply because they are afraid of all the ills it brings. Secondly, after it hurts it certainly will help; because now they are aware of the predicament they are in. Sometimes they are too close to see the wrong thinking that it is right. Lastly, it will ultimately begin to **HEAL**. I have never seen a doctor heal a disease or sickness that did not first hurt, but after it has been hurting, it begins to help and begins to heal. Let me close by asking you a question; why do you think we run from telling our friends, loved ones, constituents and others the truth sometimes? I know, because **THE TRUTH HURTS**. Go forth and begin sharing the truth with all of those we love and are committed to telling them what will usher in *Healing*.

APPLICATION SEVEN

You Have To Go Through It

Mark 4:35-37

You have to go through it! Allow me to testify. Having bad days and hard ships are really not all that popular or inviting. I would much rather experience good times than to spend any given time in bad times. The writer Mark here in our thought this week opens his expression and sharing by saying Jesus says to his boys; "**LET US PASS OVER TO THE OTHER SIDE**." Strange in some ways; but simple in other ways; It's simple because he was just telling them where they were going, but it is strange because after he tells them he goes and finds a resting place and falls asleep. Think about the best rest any person can ever have is when it's raining. But it's not raining. He has been working all day and speaking to many people and automatically falls into a sleep on the ship. Jesus says, "let us pass over to the other side" knowing that the storm was coming. You do realize that Jesus knows about the storms in your life and he wants to teach us how to sleep through a storm. He does not want you to stress in a storm He would much rather you sleep in a storm because sleeping signifies I am not worried about what is going on around me. But watch this: He already gave us the answer to the question that He knew we would answer. The storm has arisen, winds are blowing, thunder is barking, lightening is flashing and **HE'S ASLEEP**. They ask the question Jesus, Master **DON'T YOU CARE ABOUT US**. He wakes up with sleep in his eyes and immediately in His mind He has already given them the answer; think back with me. He initially said: **LET US PASS OVER TO THE OTHER SIDE**! Understand this: if He said **LET US** that means He's in it with you. If He said: **PASS OVER**; it means you won't go down. If He said: to the other side, it means: what we are in we won't die in! So in everything we go through this week, day or moment. The only reason you are in it is **YOU HAVE TO GO THROUGH IT** in order to get to the other side!

APPLICATION EIGHT

M.E. Lyons

What's Your Name?

Mark 5:2-9

What's your name? many of us have names that categorize us some are given names with specific meanings according to culture; others are given nicknames for what they have done in life, while there are some who are just labeled a name because of someone else being named the very same thing. Particularly in this scripture this man was named according to where he was. It is a dangerous thing to know that where you are in life is not a good place but still remain! Think about it; a woman is in an abusive relationship and therein threatens the safety of her children; yet remains. A man knows his wife has not been faithful to him and he does all he can to make it right but it continuously eats him away to the point that the love that he would need for future relationships have been cut away. A friend that has been there all your life but now has unbelievably took what they knew about you and used it to their benefit, and just to save face and continue saying that you are still friends hang out with the very thing that causes injury to you ; you continue to subject yourself to. The story here teaches us that we are called . . . where we are! Why stay in a place that hurts you, why go around people that mean you harm; tell me what feels good about cutting yourself? We may say but I don't cut myself; you do when you live in a place that's **NOT FOR YOU!** You see graveyards are for things that are dead; and when God allows something to die in your life it is time to move on to something living. **THAT'S YOUR CUE TO SHOUT!** Consider the question, Jesus asked this young man. Excuse me sir; but what is your name? He replied Legion, for we are many. In laymen's terms he is saying there are so many personalities, I really don't know who I am, which explains why I live among the dead. Question: **What is your name?**

APPLICATION NINE

Be Careful
Who You Kick It With!

I Corinthians 15:33

Be careful who you kick it with! You know how it is to have friends, comrades, and companions who we love to spend time with because of how laid back and cool it feels to talk with them. You seemingly have so much in common. You even have those who on your job you spend break time with and perhaps some time on Fridays going out and having dinner. Perhaps there is someone who lives in the same apartments, or lives in the same neighborhood as you and from time to time you spend time with. Could it be someone in your Church that because your families have ties from way back you spend time around them out of the long history your family has had with their family? Well if the answer is yes to any of these questions then what happens next is crucial. What do you talk about when you are with these people? As a continuation of yesterday what we say can **MESS YOU UP**. Paul writes this letter to the Corinthian Church and says to them; watch who you hang with; because who you hang with can alter who you are as a person and cause you to begin acting like who you are **NOT**! You are familiar with speaking with someone and before you know it you have become so lost in what they were saying and who they were speaking about that who you are is **NO LONGER**. Now you have become a carbon copy of who you are with! **BE WHO YOU ARE!** The only way to save face and continue to be original instead of a copy is to **WATCH WHO YOU HANG WITH** and more importantly **WATCH WHO YOU TALK TO**, the word deceived in this scripture means to roam or become seduced . . . you know when you roam it actually means going in places you did not **ORGINALLY** intend to go. Two things you should remember before you enter into conversations with ANYONE, first is that communications here simply means intercourse; WOW, I know it blew my mind too; here's what happens when we talk; the words we say produce offspring and those babies will produce other babies. DO you want what you say to be spread over town because you **LAID DOWN** (in a verbal sense) **WITH THE WRONG PERSON?** Lastly, when speaking to someone your manners are on the line; which says; YOUR HABITS take these things and share among oters. Don't let your habits be heard all over wherever you are because you chose to communicate with the wrong person. **JUST BE CAREFUL WHO YOU KICK IT WITH.**

APPLICATION TEN

It's Not All That Bad

II Corinthians 12:7-9

It's not all that bad! There as so many instances in life whereas we pray and ask God through prayer the things we need in life, and even desire in life. Be it a financial breakthrough, relationship repair, family fix, the blessing of a job or specific needs and it seems as if nothing happens or no answer is given. You struggle with whether or not the answer that I have is of God or my own mind telling me to do a certain thing. God speaks to us in times we feel that He hasn't and sometimes He says and answers in a way that we do not desire Him to. You know how it is to really petition and pray to God and need Him to show up right away only to find out that what you were looking for is not what you **GOT**. No is really not all that bad because no builds us up, it grows us up, it strengthens and it empowers us to be better and stronger than we were before we knelt before the Lord. Paul has a thorn in his flesh and comes before God and asks Him to remove this **hindrance** . . . but the truth of the matter is a **hindrance** can only help if we would learn how to **handle** it. Just as a child wants to play in the street and does not even consider the danger all around them. The parent from wherever they are says: **NO**. They are not saying no to keep their child from having fun they are saying no to protect them from the unseen and oncoming danger that is lurking. We want God to take it away and He wants us to grow in it, because after the growth we can handle the next realm He has for us. Next time you pray to God and it seems and appears as if God has not answered; reconsider because He may have already spoken but the answer you desire is not the answer you get; **IT IS NOT ALL THAT BAD!**

APPLICATION ELEVEN

Make A Choice Already

I Kings 18:21

Stop contemplating and make a choice. Every time we as believers pause wait or hesitate, we give way to the enemy! Think of it like this: Whenever we stop we only grant opportunity for the enemy to take a step because when we constantly make decisions and choose according to the will of God; we weaken and limit the chances that satan can cause us to become unstable!

APPLICATION TWELVE

It's Contagious

John 13:35

Several things in this life are contagious: which includes diseases, sicknesses, hatred, jealousy among many others. In this scripture we shall consider this week Jesus instructs all of those who claim to be family that you don't have to say anything to signify you belong to Him you have to have contracted this mentality of **L-OV-E** and once this has been running through your bloodstream; the poor are being assisted, the downtrodden are being uplifted, the downcast are being restored and the lost souls are being claimed. **WHY,** because when this love is being exemplified; your helping and loving on others becomes contagious and the process begins because when true love is shared it does not matter how you fight it has a way of being passed from person to person

My question to you is: **DO YOU HAVE IT**? I do; so watch out because it is highly contagious!

APPLICATION THIRTEEN

Are You Hungry?

Mark 8:1-3

Jesus teaches a very valuable lesson here in this scripture. He instructs the disciples of the desire to feed the multitude due to His compassion simply because of their commitment. Consider this principle; our Elder Brother Jesus goes over and above when we make our priority to spend more time with Him. He says, "I want to feed them because they have been with me **THREE DAYS**." Now understand spiritually, if you need a **WORD FROM THE LORD** concerning anything in your life and your life feels empty and spiritually your stomach is growling needing to fill that void. Spend some time with Him and **HE WILL FEED YOUR NEED!**

APPLICATION FOURTEEN

Who Is In Your Fave Five?

Mark 2:5

Simple story with a strong suggestion; be careful who you hang with because who you hang with might be who either can help or hurt you. Everyone who's in your immediate circle or square does not qualify to carry your corner!

APPLICATION FIFTEEN

What's Your Reason?

Luke13:6, 7

God is the owner of the vineyard, Jesus is the dresser of the vineyard, and we are in the tree. The question is why no fruit; God says I have given this tree everything it needs to grow but nothing is coming from it. I know that after three years there should be a bud, sprout, leaf, a sign of fruit; but I find nothing. Why is it that when people see us on our jobs, at home, in the streets, or even at Church there is no sign that we belong to God! We speak and sound like the world; dress and look like the world; live and carry on like the world and even think and plan like the world and we can never have spiritual outcomes with worldly roots.

APPLICATION SIXTEEN

What's On Your Mind?

Isaiah 26:3

This is the invitation that Facebook asks each of us consistently to accept every day all day. An invitation can be handled one of two ways it can be used for company or corruption! What takes place in the text is that as the Prophet Isaiah says; it's all about where your mind is; if your mind is not on Jesus it is a proven fact that it is on corruption. The enemy uses our idleness to post personal business, hateful expressions, expletives (curse words), explicit photos (revealing pictures) and these things cause a great divide! On the contrary if our minds are on Jesus; then we request company with Him and others cannot get to us; they might provoke you; but IT WON'T WORK! The thought I would like to place in your sagacity is: whoever you may be: Pastor, Deacon, Usher, Musician, Choir Member, First Lady, Youth or Young Adult is: WHAT'S ON YOUR MIND? If Jesus is on your mind; and you are serious about making a change; post to as many Facebook walls possible; positive an scriptural thoughts to change the World through Facebook instead of spreading hate and allowing the enemy to cloud our minds with anything that is not of God!

APPLICATION SEVENTEEN

Who Will They Find?

Jeremiah 5:1

In this scripture it instructs folk to run through the streets hurriedly and seeking to find SOMEBODY who is right. Jeremiah asks the question who can find a man of judgment and that seeks the truth not that feeds on lies and attracts wrongdoing, and is comfortable with injustice. My question to you; will you be that man or woman that they find?

APPLICATION EIGHTEEN

What Do They See When You Are Around?

Matthew 5:14

How often do those around you see light in their dark situation(s)? Or are they comfortable where they are in life when you are around? Well the simple understanding of this scripture is that if we are truly lights for Christ it will expose that which others need to change in their lives; not by what you say but by the way you live! The peculiar conception about light is: wherever light is darkness cannot stick around, because of the illumination.

APPLICATION NINETEEN

Have You Had Your Experience?

John 4:7-27

The story goes as such Jesus was speaking with this woman who had several issues and was attempting to avoid all of those who she **KNEW** was talking about her and when she gets to where she is headed she runs into someone who can fix her problem but does not realize it until He speaks to her about the situation she was in. She finally receives His Divine guidance by doing one simple thing, wait but before she does anything did you just see what happened? The disciples hate on her because they see something about to happen. Isn't that like many of those who are around us **THEY SEE** something about to break in **OUR** life and before it happens they want to **STOP** it. Stop fretting when folk hate on you and look down on you they are only **SEEING** that something is about to change in your life. Now let's press rewind and see what the woman does; she drops her water pot because she finally figured it out; sometimes you need to drop what you are doing to go tell somebody else what just went down in your life, especially when what you have been doing has not been working!

APPLICATION TWENTY

I Know The Password

Psalm 89:15

I KNOW THE PASSWORD. One translation as it relates to this passage says: blessed are the people who know the passwords of praise, who shout on parade in the bright presence of God. It is our own fault to walk around, sit around, and lay around depressed, in the dumps and discouraged when all we need to realize is that we have the password. Whatever it is that you have went through, will go through, or are in right now the Psalmist says, "It is a blessing to know how to excite and incite the Lord in whatever shape that we are in." Many times we go through our days at work and several things get under our skin; perhaps it is a co-worker who we know that does not take part in their share of the work but are just riding the waves, or a supervisor or boss who is always on you about something and every day you come in you come in with a positive attitude but it is altered by a bad attitude. Perhaps it could be a spouse or mate who does not pull their own weight and will not meet you half ways with anything or a child who no matter how much you say or how hard you try they **DO NOT** hear what you have to say well the good news is you have a **PASSWORD**. A password?

Yes, a password; you do know what a password does don't you? It gets you into places you otherwise had no access to. We say all the time when worship is going on; **<u>GET UP</u>** and praise the Lord. On the contrary many continue to sit down, but there is a secret I wish to share with you. This password works *EVERYWHERE*. So whatever you do, wherever you are; **USE YOUR PASSWORD**. When someone starts tripping on you; **USE YOUR PASSWORD**. When somebody mistreats you; **USE YOUR PASSWORD**. When you know you were right; instead of going off; **USE YOUR PASSWORD**. Because using your password *<u>(PRAISE)</u>* causes God to do something about **WHATEVER** you are in. So if you have to sneak to the break room, bathroom, car, closet, whisper, sing or pray your password. Watch how **LIGHT** comes to an otherwise **DARK** situation.

APPLICATION
TWENTY-ONE

NADA

Romans 8:38-39

NADA; we have heard this term used many times; especially in the Hispanic community. The term is used to suggest that whatever is being spoken of is empty; there is nothing there or simply blank! Paul lifts the same thought pattern for us in this passage of scripture. I begin to think of all the things that happen in life that seem to depress and suppress my spirit and keep me from my destiny, hardships, heartaches, lies, arguments and wrong decisions among many other things and they strive to cause us to struggle on a daily basis. It seems like if it aint one thing it's another! But here there are some instances Paul brings up that are shouting points because they speak to everyday living. He says nothing that is living or dead, angelic or demonic, high or low, thinkable or unthinkable, today or tomorrow, absolutely **NADA** can come between me and God. Well, you might ask what do you mean get between? I am glad you asked; a quarrel between you and a friend; or you and a loved one will sometimes cause you not to pray because you are too angry. A fight or disagreement with a child will cause you to say things that you ought not to say. Perhaps, you are worried about some business you have to take care of next week. Well first worrying is a sin and anything that you worry about puts space between you and God. Maybe that did not stop at your doorstep. What about somebody with a bad attitude? Getting back at them only pushes God further away; nothing you can imagine should ever separate you from the presence of God. This is why Paul says, **I AM CONVINCED** that **NADA** will cause me to slip up and let IT keep me from Him because He has shown me His love. Think about it very clearly! The **M.O.** for the enemy is to use people and things to cause us to create space between us and God; for when this happens we are vulnerable to his attack. So when people try to push your buttons; **NADA**. When something has come up and you really don't know how it will be taken care of; think **NADA**. When tomorrow is not here, and today has not finished; think about **NADA**. Oh and when the unthinkable happens and you want to scream; think **NADA**. Why; because **NOTHING, NADA, ZILCH, ZERO**, nothing should separate you or create space between you and your God!

APPLICATION
TWENTY-TWO

Who Is Carrying Your Corner?

Mark 2

Simple question today, whoever you have carrying your corner has power to take you where they want to go and not where you desire to go. Do your friends have your best interest at heart?

APPLICATION
TWENTY-THREE

Don't Miss Your Blessing

Luke 17

Don't miss your blessing! Many times in life we believe in God because we have acquired a new ride, a luxurious home or an extra check that we have fallen into a real blessing, but not so; what we have inside is far more important than any external and material thing. We have a propensity and proclivity to measure our blessings from what we get instead of what we have. This is the case in this story. Ten men are traveling together; **ONLY** because they have something in common! Now understand there is a life application here; because some people only use where they are in life to get something better and often times the springboard they use is **YOU**. They hang with you because there is something different about you. You act a little strange, you walk a little different and they see an opportunity to use you for where they feel they need to go in life. I have a question that the spirit of God just placed in my spirit. Have you ever asked yourself why these brothers hung out together? I mean they were from different backgrounds, different ethnicities, different cultures but common circumstances had them in the very same predicament. I need to hurrily tell you that were you are right now are not by happenstance. These brothers hung together because 90 percent of them wanted to be healed but they did not want to be whole. You see what happens in life is everybody that hangs around you is not there because they genuinely care. Some people are there because there is something different about you and if they see it why don't you? Watch what happens; Jesus shows up and **THEY** scream; **LORD HAVE MERCY <u>ON US</u>**: did you just hear that? They say on us because they realize that something in the us could benefit them individually. It is a blessing for others to see something in you that would cause someone who would not regularly hang around you to do so, because they need something from **HIM**. So let them hang around you; so what they may be using your gift, anointing and love for God. Hopefully their contact with you will cause contact with God. Not to mention the one who had the relationship went back and said thank you and for that he was made whole. Last point and we will conclude. Whole in Greek means to protect; the blessing was just external but when Jesus saw that it was that was real He gave them an internal blessing. He said you are protected; otherwise **I GOT YOUR BACK**!

APPLICATION
TWENTY-FOUR

Can You Fill In The Blank?

Psalms 23:1

The Psalmist says, "The Lord is" and almost leaves us on a cliff until he personalizes and gives us room to meditate and ponder that He is not only a myriad of things to David but He can be the same and much more to us. Can you answer the question? When trouble, famine, circumstances, situations arise where does HE fit in your blank? The Lord is **MY**_____!

APPLICATION
TWENTY-FIVE

Built For The Road Ahead

Isaiah 43:2

It sometimes seems as if everything that can go wrong; does go wrong! If it's not your car acting up; it's your family members mistreating you; or your money is funny and many other things that take place. We almost live by the creed; if it's not one thing it's another. Well, Isaiah has a remedy and explanation of this seemingly consistent problem. He teaches us that whatever it is that we as Christians go through. **WE ARE BUILT FOR THE ROAD AHEAD**. Listen to what he says: when you go through the water; **I AM THERE**. When you go through the rivers; **I WILL BE WITH YOU**. When thou go through the fire; **YOU WONT BE BURNED**. Read this carefully and we are going to shout together; when he says waters he pluralizes it buy saying that no matter how many things try and drown you; **THEY CANNOT**. When they splash in your face; it will take your breath away but you **WONT DIE**; think about it if you are anything like me when water runs over my head it feels like I may be drowning and it takes away my breath, but the fact of the matter is, **I AM STILL ALIVE**, then he moves on to say, **RIVERS** but in my thoughts at first rivers are occupied by water so why repeat. It is not repetitive; the difference is rivers have currents, and currents grab whatever it is that is in it and carry it to where it wants to. But he encourages us by saying whatever it is that seemingly takes you in every direction, and tosses you through and fro; you will not be lost at sea. Then he says even through the fire; it will not burn you; very simple; what may seems hot will only help. While you are dealing with situations that seem unbearable; remember. **YOU ARE BUILT FOR THE ROAD AHEAD!** Be it: your marriage, friendship, job, mind, home, finances, children, family, Church or your life. **YOU ARE BUILT FOR THE ROAD AHEAD!**

APPLICATION
TWENTY-SIX

How Blessed
Do You Want To Be?

Matthew 5:7

This question unveils how much we either resemble God or are rebellious of God. The writer here says, "We are blessed when we are full of mercy." What is mercy? Mercy is the ability to see and feel the pain, mishap or situation that someone else is in as if it were you! So instead of looking down on someone, make this week a practice of looking down to help up and there you will find your blessing. When you read headlines in the local newspaper; **BE MERCIFUL**. When you hcar gossip on someone else; **BE MERCIFUL**. When you catch someone doing what they should not be doing; **BE MERCIFUL**. When your child only repeats what you have done when you were that age; **BE MERCIFUL**. Blessed are the merciful; for they shall obtain mercy!

APPLICATION
TWENTY-SEVEN

Have A Seat

James 1:2, 3

Isn't awkward that James the half brother of Jesus would suggest for us to be happy in heartache? We seem to deal with many challenges on a daily basis that more than not attempt to discourage us. It is my belief; bad things happen to good people so those who do not know the Lord will be able to see the Jesus in us so they will find CHRIST for themselves! I know it's not the most popular statement: **BUT WE GO THROUGH** so others can see Christ! Far too many times we become faint and give up and the message and signal it sends is that we express that God cannot handle the situation. Watch the pattern of the text before us this day; James says: Count it **ALL** joy; <u>**STOP**</u>. What does James mean **COUNT**. Well, I am super satisfied you inquired! He uses the word Count because in the Greek language it literally means command or think. Do you know what our biggest obstacle is when something goes wrong or awry? **IT IS OUR THINKING**. I have noticed some of us have contracted the very same sickness. This sickness is our thinking. The first thing we do when something happens that **WE THINK** is unfixable is: we begin to **THINK** negatively! Oh, my money has become a little short, my car is not running right, my relationship is dysfunctional, my job won't cut it; complaint after complaint! What this encouraging writer has simply shared with us is that we have to correct our thinking. Why think negative when we serve a positive God? So, he suggests for us to command ourselves to make our minds produce joy even in non enjoyable situations! So what the bills are due; keep your joy. So what they are talking about you; keep your joy. So what they hate on you; keep your joy. The saints of old used to sing: "This joy that I have the world didn't give it to me; and the world didn't give and the world can't take it away." They were only singing what James had already said. The last thing James prescribes for us to learn is that what this all does is cause us to have more patience. If you are anything like me; **YOUR PATIENCE NEEDS WORK**! What better way to build your patience level than to allow divers temptations and troubles show up unexpectedly and then sit back and see how we handle the WAIT. The question, I would like to ask you and then ask you to ask someone else as encouragement is; ***HOW WILL YOU HANDLE YOUR WAIT?***

APPLICATION
TWENTY-EIGHT

When Will Your Season Be?

I Peter 5:6

Here in the scripture that is before us Peter throws a curve ball our way and has the answer given before the question is answered. He tells us that if we learn to be humble; we shall be exalted. Then he turns around and tacks a three letter word on to the question-like presentation. He says, "In DUE time", which in Greek means season or occasion. He tells us is that we can go to the next level only by humbling ourselves and to be in subjection to God. Otherwise, TOTALLY sold out. That is not all he suggests; he then says in DUE time. I really do not want you to miss this; in laymen terms he literally says it is all up to you when you are exalted. My question to you is: when will your season begin?

APPLICATION
TWENTY-NINE

Where Are Your Seeds?

Matthew 13:1-9

This parable speaks of Jesus resting by the sea; only just to share with those who would listen. He speaks to them about **SEEDS** and after He speaks to them about **SEEDS** He speaks to them about securing. Many times people come to Church and hear the **SEEDS**, but the problem is the **SECURITY** of the **SEEDS**. We hear messages of hope; but still leave disheartened. We hear sermons of commitment; but leave disconnected. We hear sermons of salvation; but leave lost. We even hear messages of cleansing; but leave tainted. Why, you may ask? The problem is: we hear **SEEDS**; but it is up to you to secure the **SEEDS**! My question to you is: **WHAT ARE YOU DOING WITH YOUR** seeds?

APPLICATION THIRTY

You Can Win
With A Bad Hand

Mark 3:1-5

You can win with a bad hand! I grew up with great expectation ready to go to family functions because I knew I would be afforded the opportunity of experiencing my uncles, aunts, cousins, and even some friends of the family crowded around a card table playing spades. They would talk noise one to another and occasionally I had an uncle named, "Uncle Junior" and he was a Pastor of a Church for many years, but when it came to playing cards and dominoes he took that very serious! Sometimes he would tell his partner after a hand has been played; that if they had a bad hand; don't give up; remember you have a partner! I could stop right there. Beloved, realize that **WHATEVER** it is that you are dealt in life; **YOU HAVE A PARTNER**! I have had my share of ups and downs, but the older I become the more I realize that playing with a bad hand is not really all that bad. The reason a bad hand is not as bad as it seems, because it teaches us how to be a better player when we do get a good hand! This scripture for consideration points out some very critical messages. Notice how

Jesus approaches this situation. He instructs the man to **STAND FORTH**, otherwise, get up, straighten up, stop sobbing; it's not what you think. Then after He tells the young man to rise up and stand up He then literally tells him to **EXTEND** that which you thought was useless. If I was in Church on Sunday morning I would tell you to lean over and tell your neighbor what Jesus was really saying here is: **PLAY YOUR HAND**, it may look bad; but play it anyhow. It may appear that because you have no spades you won't win this hand; but play it anyhow. I know you do not have any lead cards but play it anyhow. You see just because you don't have them; doesn't mean I don't. Just **STRETCH FORTH THINE HAND**; in other words **PLAY THE HAND YOU WERE DEALT** and as your partner I will take care of the lightweight!

APPLICATION
THIRTY-ONE

Do You Really Have A Pass?

Romans 6:1

There are passes seemingly to everything in life; allowances to travel through toll ways, allowances to get in a movie or show free and even proverbial passes to get out of trouble! However, there are truly no passes to sin and not be punished for our wrong doings. Paul shares a very important and imperative point with us in this verse and that is that ALL wrongs have no passes! Listen, to what he says: Should we keep on doing what we have been doing because grave seems to overshadow sin? Otherwise, it's like a puny wrestler taking on a massive bodybuilder and Roman wrestler. Many feel because sin has no authority over grace that it will be OK to keep on sinning because God will forgive us! My question to you is: "Do you really have a pass?"

APPLICATION
THIRTY-TWO

Have You Graduated?

John 15:1-7

Have you graduated? Isn't it a good feeling to complete a certain thing in life and know that after all the hard work, it has now paid off because you are ready to start the next chapter in your life? It may be graduating from high school, graduating from college, or even graduating from a specific stage in life. There are always THINGS in life that are eligible for graduation. This scripture(s) prescribes and exclaims that in our personal lives; **GRADUATION IS NECESSARY**! We encompass a great deal of circumstances and situations in this walk of life that we should not have to deal with if we would only acquiesce to **graduating rather than being satisfied in remedial**. Let me explain: John says that Jesus said that He is the true vine and first thing is that every branch *(which is us . . .)* in **HIM** that **WILL NOT** bear fruit **HE TAKETH AWAY**. Notice, He suggests that if He does not see a change in your life there is **NO USE FOR YOU!** <u>**WOW**</u>, What a bold statement; if you display no change; why keep you around? I am not sure about you but I do not want to be removed because of my display; I want to graduate. Now get this, watch the pyramid of progression in this series of scriptures. He first says fruit, **MORE** fruit, and then **MUCH FRUIT**! There is a lesson plan in this scripture and that is why you remain in the remedial course and keep going over things you have your entire life and exempt yourself from graduation. Many people question and wonder why is it that I am still dealing with the same issues I have been for **YEARS**! Why am I still the only one in the marriage trying to make it work? Why is it that I cannot find a better job? I want to start a business; but nothing is working in my favor. Why can I not find someone to love me for who I am? Many more questions have been asked. Well, I have a suggestion; perhaps you are more satisfied unconsciously in staying in the remedial course than you are in graduation. Fruit in this presentation is not to maintain it is to multiply! Many people are content maintaining their fruit than multiplying their fruit. Well, Pastor how can I multiply my fruit? It's easy do **MORE**! **More** Love, **More** Concern, **More** Commitment to Christ, **More** Prayer, **More** Consecration, **More** Personal Bible Study, **More** of the Word, **More** of what **CHRIST** has asked for me to do. Getting to the point being Remedial means that we don't want to do **MORE** . . . because we have to give up MORE! It's in the text; every now and again even when we graduate; HE has to cut and prune because in growth there is always some **THINGS** (and People) that will hinder your growth and graduation! So in all of this that has been said; *"Are you prepared for graduation?"*

APPLICATION
THIRTY-THREE

Your Time Is Coming

Hebrews 13: 5

Your time is coming; or is it? There are times in all of our lives whereas we look at others accoutrements achievements and even accomplishments and question why is it that I do not have what they have. This question at some point and time has arisen in every person's life about any given thing. Your question may have come about because someone got a new car and you know that they have not been struggling as long as you have with transportation. It might be a spouse that someone was blessed to have and your question is rooted out of jealousy because you wanted them first. Perhaps, it may be a lifestyle someone around you has, and your question is not about the situation they have but to God; why is it they are living like this and I have been doing the right thing for years. **ALL** of us have asked a question similar to these above. *WHY? WHY? WHY?* This is not a time to focusing on the why it is a time to focusing on the **WHO** . . . after all; when it is all said and done. Focusing on the why will only upset, frustrate, and cause us to live very jealous and hateful lives . . . however focusing on the **WHO** causes us to look and stay focused on the one who can eventually grant us our requests, notice the operative word *EVENTUALLY*.

In this scripture, the Hebrew writer says stop wanting what other people have; stop hating on them because they have more than you. The truth is you have enough for your level right now. Now get this: when the writer uses the word content here it suggests that what you have is enough; *I KNOW; PLAIN AND SIMPLE* but you missed it! He says he will never give your experience more than you need. What would happen if a ship had **TOO MUCH CARGO**? It would sink. What would happen if a plane had too many engines? **IT WOULD PLUMMET**. What would happen if we had **TOO MANY THINGS**? We wouldn't serve Him. He literally says when your mind matures; your money matures, when your apprehension has been positively altered; your possessions will not be presented until your character has not been compromised. Your life will not be lifted. Can you hear him saying, don't talk about a person's things and life as if you want theirs, just be happy with what you have, because I will never leave you nor forsake you. Otherwise as long as I am with you; **YOU HAVE EVERYTHING YOU NEED**! My question to you is: **"What do you want?"**

APPLICATION
THIRTY-FOUR

What Are You Waiting For?

John 2:5

Many times in life the Lord has instructed us to do something and we contemplate, procrastinate, and hold reservations as to whether or not we are prepared or have the necessary tools; when all we are to acquiesce to is; **DO IT**! So as we suggest to you this day is whatever it is God has told you to do; do it. Preach, sing., love, help, pray, encourage or be there for someone. Hang in there and make it work. Don't give up; **DO IT** and the end result will **ALWAYS** be he has saved the **BEST FOR LAST**.

APPLICATION
THIRTY-FIVE

How Much Do You Love?

John 3:16

This scripture is one we all remember for some reason or another; Sunday school, vacation bible school or just by happenstance! God here says I love you so much that I want to give you something; I do not want to give you scraps, I want you to have the best. Leftovers would not be enough, and regifting would not suffice! I love you **SO** much I want to go broke displaying my love! So I gave you my **ONLY** Son. Beloved **TRUE LOVE** has a tendency to bankrupt you sometimes!

APPLICATION
THIRTY-SIX

Get Focused

Romans 8:28

You are looking at the wrong thing! How often our eyes are strapped, stayed and stuck on the bad? I mean to never seem to see anything good happen in our lives is almost depressing and discouraging. You know how it is; you may be out enjoying the company of friends and for some reason you cannot **SMILE** or laugh because your mental eyes are focused on a car note that is due without the privilege of the money to accompany it, or a fight you just had with a loved one . . . and **SMILING** or laughing is almost difficult to force because of where your eyes are affixed. It is a very disturbing feeling to struggle to get into worship when your mental eyes are glued to the **HELL** you are going through and for someone to say Praise the Lord or Come on it's not as bad as it seems somehow worsens your situations because you are in the situation and they are not. There happens to be a solution in the writing of Paul in this twenty-eighth verse of the eighth chapter. I want to slip you a spiritual sedative if you would allow me. Paul instantly says: and we know. Wait Paul; **WE**, I am in this all by myself; what do you mean **WE**? Paul says **WE** because he understands **YOU ARE NOT IN IT**

ALONE. **WE,** means Christians. **WE** meaning God. You should know that **ALL** things work together for good of them who are the called. Now here is the spiritual sedative; the word **TO**. You missed your shout! Paul actually slips in the Spiritual Sedative in the word **TO**; he literally says God only gives the good stuff **TO** them that **LOVE** Him. Well Paul what about the rest; I am glad you asked! You have to be called according to His purpose. How does that apply to me? **CALLED** in Greek means **INVITED**, while Purpose in the Greek language means **HIS** place. You should be shouting right now. You will get the Spiritual Sedative if you are invited to His place. When you are a child of the King he will give you everything you need; if you are on the **V.I.P.** list! I don't want you to forget the instruction though; you are looking at one thing (bad and sad) when you should be looking at **ALL** things that is where it works out for your good. I want to ask you a crucial question: What are you looking at?

APPLICATION
THIRTY-SEVEN

Don't Give Up Too Soon

Galatians 6:9

Don't give up too soon! Far too many times, I see people stand in lines forever and a day and then after their patience has been worn they turn around and leave out of frustration and I look at them and notice; they walked away, and they were **NEXT IN LINE.** Why wait forever and walk away when you get to the counter? Well, that is the theme of this scripture we examine today. And let us not be weary in well doing: for in due season we shall reap, if we faint not. Consider for a moment why we think that **WAITING** causes us to become **WEARY.** Waiting is a blessing when we consider what waiting means; it means that we are either on standby for something we have desired, or it is a thing that we are anticipating an answer. Either way the misunderstood concept here is that why walk away from something that is potentially the best for us. Beloved, the writer here ties verse eight to verse nine by telling us to stop thinking in the flesh and begin thinking in the spirit; because he then says **AND** (which ties the two together) and says **DON'T GIVE UP TOO SOON**. If you must wait stay in the line; hang in there; cry if you must but do not walk away because you shall reap. **STOP!** What does reap mean to me; it means you shall get; you shall receive. You shall be rewarded. So all I need to do is just learn how to **WAIT**, and my **WANT** will be given if you can just **HOLD ON**! Your turn is coming. Lastly, he says; it is contingent upon your mentality; if you faint not. The word faint connotes Relaxation. Take this under consideration and we will make this principle applicable **TODAY**. I know Paul says **FAINT**; but in modern terms he literally says CHILL OUT, it is going to happen! So what my inquiring mind would like to know is: **ARE YOU REALLY GONG TO GIVE UP YOUR PLACE IN LINE THAT EASY?**

APPLICATION
THIRTY-EIGHT

He Is Waiting On You
Hebrew 11:1

Upon reading this verse and reciting it for years and years; most of the focus of this verse is placed on the faith when faith is only the object of His intent, in essence the focus and object of the scripture is **NOW**! We believe that we are waiting on God most times when in reality He is waiting on us; how you might ask? This is evident because Faith is not about tomorrow; it is not about yesterday, and faith is not even applicable to the future. **FAITH** is only usable **NOW**. The expiration date is right now! Through all of your heartache, questions, concerns, unpleasantries, and uncertainties activate your faith **NOW**! My question to you is: What are you waiting on?

APPLICATION
THIRTY-NINE

Can We All Just Get Along?

Luke 15

CAN WE ALL JUST GET ALONG? This was a cliché put out many years ago and it was coined to suggest that there is far too much confusion to make any progress. If we are to be honest with ourselves concerning our community, states, and world; many have come to find out there is a myriad of division that needs to be eradicated so that unity can prevail! One of the most prolific and memorable parables in the Bible and more personally is that of the prodigal son. Nearing the placement of the prodigal son is the parable of the lost coin. These three parables that are mentioned backed to back are suggestively synchronized teaches us the principle of working together. How; you may ask let me show you. In this parable, the Physician Luke speaks of a woman who lost a coin; **SILVER** coin and **SWEPT** the whole house until it is found. Initially I need to share with you that she uses a **BROOM.** To find the coin is simple you might say. There is great significance to the broom because in an abbreviated synopsis of this text the broom has bristles on the one end that is used to gather that which has congested or dirtied the place needing cleaning. If you have not noticed a broom has

98

long bristles, short bristles, dirty bristles, clean bristles, bended bristles, straight bristles, big bristles, small bristles, wide bristles and even skinny bristles, but altogether they can reach anything that is hidden or out of sight! Our ultimate goal as Christians on this proverbial and spiritual broom is to reach **EVERYONE EVERYWHERE**. We cannot do this separate or apart! We must work together because the old cannot reach **EVERYONE** without the young, and likewise the young cannot reach **EVERYONE** without the old. The truth of the matter is **WE ALL** must work together to make a change and reach every crevice, crack, crook and cranny! So, as you go throughout your day, week, month, or year strive to work together with others so we can **SWEEP THE NATION** by offering whatever it is your bristle was created to do!

APPLICATION FORTY

What's On Your Record?

Malachi 3:8-12

What's **on** your record? Whoa, most times when the scripture is read there is silence, and wall put up. There they go again with that money scripture. What do they need money for now? Well, beloved let me pose the question to you another way: "How many convictions are on your record?" In our society, having a record can hinder you from getting a job, getting a place to live, and may hinder you from hanging around certain people. The issue that many of us struggle with is the fact that the ones with the record are not bad people they were just in the wrong place at the wrong time or made a bad decision. All in all they are good people, respectful and for the most part do the right things in life. The irony of this whole situation is little do we know many of us are walking around with a long laundry list of convictions and not even know it. Many of us have caused our misdemeanors to turn into felonies! How? I will share it with you in that which is to follow. The writer here starts this familiar scripture off in an abrupt way: **WILL A MAN ROB GOD**? Then he answers just as quickly as he asks; **YES!** You see robbery and theft are two separate crimes. Theft is when you sneak

101

and take something, whereas **ROBBERY** is sometimes in the broad day light and you take it from their face. What he does is tell us when we do not pay what we owe in tithes and give what we should in offering we are **ROBBING GOD** not man, not the Pastor, not the Deacons; we are **ROBBING GOD**. Quickly consider what he says happens when we **ROB HIM**; we began to be cursed. Otherwise, you make **HIM** sick to **HIS** stomach and **HE** can no longer look at you. That's when your record follows you: you pray for a blessing, new car, new home, good man, good woman, peace of mind, children to behave correctly, family problems, and **NOTHING HAPPENS, WHY?** HE is not looking our way. The convictions that are on our records catch up to us. Then he turns the tables; and says: **IF** you do these things; I will **BLESS** you so much you will not have means to contain it. He will cause that or them which desire to see you consumed; to stand by and watch you **BE BLESSED!** Then he says and everybody will know you are **BLESSED**. Take note that we **PAY** our **TITHES** and we give our **OFFERINGS**. We owe **OUR** tithes **TO** God; but **OFFERING** is just what it is what we think of **HIM** our offering! So when we begin to make excuses about **WHY** we don't have enough to **PAY** your tithes and **GIVE** your offerings; think about the **MANY CONVICTIONS** going on our records! The time will come when we withhold that which God knows we have and our **RECORD** will catch up to us. Little do we know that we are holding a proverbial **GUN** to God's face saying: give me everything you have when we continually ask him for **THINGS** and never give **HIM** what He deserves? Question: How many counts of **ROBBERY** are you willing to put on your record before you give up the lifestyle of **ROBBERY**?

APPLICATION
FORTY-ONE

What Are You In?

Job 1:22

Job was troubled seemingly from every corner of his life, but yet and still he trusted in God. Job never gave up, never quit trusting; he became a little shaky but he knew God had everything in control! When we encounter situations that we cannot understand, nor control; will it be said of us that **WE SINNED NOT, NOR CHARGED GOD FOOLISHLY?** My question to you: Will we be an example when we get **IN**?

APPLICATION
FORTY-TWO

Your Prescription Has Been Filled

Proverbs 17:22

Your prescription has been filled! There are several organs within the body; but the heart is one of the most vital of all organs. Through and with the heart one has the organ that pumps life through every vein and vessel of their body. We have many things in life that causes different things to take place in our hearts; both spiritually and physically, but the most important one is in the spiritual. I can point out a few: someone has upset us for some unknown reason and it causes an angry heart; we call it our blood boiling! Then there is when someone has mistreated us or betrayed us and it causes a sad heart and we have deemed this as a broken heart. There is also the possibility of someone we love passing away or being taken away from us whether through imprisonment or because we can no longer reach out to them; which is a lonely we call this an empty heart. There are also instances whereas our hearts can be affected in the physical because of the absence of the spiritual. The writer here almost **PRESCRIBES A MEDICATION** for any heart condition; be it spiritual or physical.

Solomon says, "A merry heart doeth good like **a** medicine." Did you catch that? He said like **A** medicine as if to suggest that are so many medicinal options out there but it is your choice of which one you will take! There is the prescription of alcohol to satisfy. Then there are those who use the prescription of other physical enhancements to satisfy. Many choose option of pity parties, depression or even thoughts of suicide. But Solomon's says: the choice is yours. You know when a Doctor prescribes a medicine; he/she cannot force you to take it, the choice is yours. The truth is, if you take it; your chance of recovery is much greater! As Solomon writes this prescription for us to have it filled, he then shares our diagnosis. The diagnosis is, a **BROKEN SPIRIT**! It was there all along, and do you know what a broken spirit is? It is **DEPRESSION, STRESS** and **FRUSTRATION**. **MISERY** and one other scholar say that a broken spirit is simply: **HEAVINESS OF HEART**! So with this **DOCTOR'S** visit behind you . . . what was your prognosis? I know my choice will be to follow the Doctor's orders! My question to you: **HAVE YOU TAKEN YOUR MEDICINE**?

APPLICATION
FORTY-THREE

Today Is The Day

Matthew 6: 34

Today is the day! How many times do we spend our mornings contemplating on something that we are to do today and by the end of us thinking about that which we are to do, we come to the conclusion that we will do it tomorrow or next week? There are numerous times in my own life; I have a myriad of tasks and places to go and because of the congestion of our schedule we make up in our mind to put off some of the things today for tomorrow! What an indictment that is to plan for the unknown! Really think about it; many have made plans to do things next year, next month, next week and even tomorrow, not knowing whether or not tomorrow is promised to us! That's a **GIVEN** I know; but the reality is: who knows what tomorrow may bring! It could bring sickness, a broken marriage, a fractured friendship, a child who made the wrong decision and has now been incarcerated or even death! Scary as it may seem it should open our eyes. **TOMORROW IS NOT PROMISED TO US**! Many people hate to speak about the inevitable but no matter who we are, how much money we have or do not have, what our last names are, or how sick or well we are. **TOMORROW HOLDS THE**

UNKOWN! What are we saying? We are simply saying why not bury the hatchet with that person you have been spending countless nights and hours; trying to figure out what happened! Start doing what we know we should be doing . . . work at your marriage **NOW** instead of **WAITING UNTIL IT IS TOO LATE**. Spend the necessary time with your children that they so rightfully deserve, become more committed to Christ as we know we should. Start investing in others so that when it is your turn the return will be **GREATER**. Let **TODAY** begin a life that is not frustrated with the worries of **TOMORROW** but filled with **<u>POSSIBILITIES</u>** of **TODAY**! My question to you: **WILL TODAY BE YOUR DAY**?

APPLICATION
FORTY-FOUR

Now; Who's The Judge?

Matthew 7:1

Isn't it awfully odd how so many want to grade your papers in life and never realize the flaws on their papers proverbially? Others can always see your blemishes but never your beauty or good! We have all at one point in our lives fallen victim to sitting behind a judge's bench and condemning others as we have contracted selective amnesia on what we have done in life! So my question to you: Are we qualified to judge?

APPLICATION
FORTY-FIVE

Don't Stay Out Too Late!

Matthew 25:1-12

Don't stay out too late! One of the greatest misnomers in our time spiritually is that we have forever to do what we desire to do. Sowing your wild oats, have fun; you are young. When you get ready you can come on in! But the problem with this thinking is **TIME** waits on no man/woman. Have you ever considered that our Father in Heaven most times is waiting on us to come in? I remember when we were young and my brother would go out to parties unannounced or my sister would sneak out and my father had a way of staying up as late as it would take to make sure that when they returned he was the welcoming party! When we do the very same thing as it relates to doing our own thing and saying; I will always have tomorrow or time enough to do the right thing what actually happens is God sits up waiting to see when we come in what will be our excuse. I want to submit to you beloved that **you** may stay out too late. In the case of these sisters the record is five of them were wise and five were foolish and the foolish figured **TIME WOULD WAIT ON THEM**. What actually happens is that they took for granted that originally they were in the right place; but they were not

115

prepared to **STAY**! **WOW**, what a great feeling it is to be in Church on Sundays (the right place) because we figure we have plenty of time to get **REAL SERIOUS** we are not prepared to stay. We slip off doing things we should not be doing. We spend more time **SLIPPING AWAY** than **STAYING IN**. These five foolish women wanted to mooch off of those who were Serious than becoming serious enough themselves . . . watch what happens: they leave and are now locked out! I don't know about you but at the Lyons' home if you continuously stayed out too late: soon you were locked out and getting in was no option; you would have to find another place to sleep. My question to you: **WHERE WILL YOU SLEEP TONIGHT**?

APPLICATION
FORTY-SIX

What Are You Chasing?

Matthew 6:33

What are you chasing? Far too often we stress, and are highly frustrated due to the fact that what we desire is not taking place in our lives. We want more money, better vehicles, bigger homes, more extravagant lifestyles, fame and fortune but spend most of the time we have been allotted to us attempting to obtain these things whether collectively or individually and many times we come up depressingly short; and then we wonder why it has not taken place! One of the most obvious problems in this high speed chase regarding things in our lives is the issue of **DIRECTION**. The most operative and important word in this scripture is: **BUT** it actually means about face, turn around, go in the opposite direction! When we stop and consider we will see the most apparent problem in lives that have not and cannot obtain the things they have set before them is they are traveling in the wrong direction. A few things are evident here: going the wrong direction you may get where you desire to be but it will take **ALL** around the world through all sorts of trials and tribulations before you ever get there. Secondly, going in the wrong direction may introduce you to places you were not supposed to pass through; **BUT**

since you desired to use your **GPS** against the **DIRECTION** He has desired for us causes more grief! Consider the suggestion Matthew gives to us: he says **BUT** seek (chase after) the Kingdom of God and His righteousness and **ALL** of these things will be **ADDED** unto you. Watch how he shares with us that the first step in obtaining what we desire is to change **DIRECTIONS**. Thirdly, he says there needs to be a **SWTICH-UP,** in other words rather than doing what you please, start doing what God wants us to do concerning the Kingdom; meaning go to Church more, give more, love more, forgive more, help more, follow more. Next, your **DESTINATION** will be realized, which yields the outcome of what seemed so distant is now so close but get this: he still says' **ADDED**; **WOW**! Add here in this scripture means: what you were once chasing after will now be chasing after you; no matter where you go: what you once desired now desires you! Otherwise, you do not have to look for them; they will look for you!

APPLICATION
FORTY-SEVEN

Who Is In Your Corner?

Mark 2: 1-6

We have heard so many times: that just because a person is in your company does not mean they are in your corner, how true that statement is! In this particular pericope, we see much truth to this cliché. This man was sick and truly needed assistance; but he just did not need assistance in the physical he needed support in the spiritual and this is exactly what took place! The record holds that the deciding factor of why this man was healed was because who was in his corner. When He saw THEIR faith; He then looks at the sick man and says: Son thy sins be forgiven thee! So my question to you: Are you in good company?

APPLICATION
FORTY-EIGHT

Do You Have
Chewing Gum Religion?

II Timothy 4:3

Do you have a chewing gum religion?
I have heard so many times during Church
someone to get up and make remarks and say:
I felt so good in Church and I left feeling even
better! I to have a good feeling while in Church
and after Church is not bad, but it is not all
the way right either! I know when we come
to Church we look for and expect to have our
burdens lifted, but there is a flip side to all of
the feelings and circumstances. I would like to
suggest a few indicators of coming to Church
with the wrong mentality will ultimately do!
Notice that Paul is speaking to Timothy; and
this particular passage and more importantly
book(s) of the Bible is speaking to the Preacher.
Listen to what he says: There will come a
time when the people will not endure **SOUND
DOCTRINE**. Now, what does that mean? In
the original language and translation these two
words collectively mean: healthy instruction.
You know this is something that we think not of
when it comes to Church we want to have the
choir sing us happy, deacons pray us happy, and
the Preacher preach us happy; but there is an

issue here! **HEALTHY INSTRUCTION** is not always **WELCOMED INFORMATION**! We would much rather hear a sermon or message that will tickle our fancy or make us feel good about the problem we are dealing with; but many times in order to get to that point we must understand that oft times the reason we are where we are is because of always desiring something that makes us feel good. Sometimes we need to hear something that will call us to the carpet! Think about this: chewing gum is a thing many use to take their minds off of something else; be it smoking, drinking or anything for that matter. We use it to freshen up what is most repulsive. We use chewing gum to bring something sweet to an otherwise sour situation. The problem with chewing gum is when the sweetness has left we normally spit it out! This is how many of us are: we will listen, adhere, and apply the Word of God as long as it is sweet and then when it seemingly has lost that sweet accompaniment we spit it out! Do not let the Word of God be the same to your life! Take the entire Bible and allow it to give **HELPFUL HINTS** to make you a better person. The Word of God is really not **CHEWING GUM** but rather it is like medicine, a pill and we must take it in order to ward and fight off **ALL** the ills of life; it may taste all that good: but it is what we need. I have a question for you: Would you rather have **CHEWING GUM** or the **PILL**?

APPLICATION
FORTY-NINE

It's Not What
It's Cracked Up To Be

Proverbs 23:17, 18

Many times people spend a multiplicity of their time looking at what others have and begin to become highly envious, and will even inquire of how to obtain what someone else has, but this wise man Solomon suggests the exact opposite; do not even look their way; focus on the Lord. The truth of the matter is looking at **STUFF** will only cause grief, but looking at the **SAVIOR** will yield a **GUARANTEE**! Because verse eighteen says: This is where your future is; it is in spending some quality time with the Savior. That is the **GUARANTEE**. The end result will be that you will not be left with a handful of problems. My question to you: Who are you looking at?

APPLICATION FIFTY

Make Sure You Dot
Your i's And Cross Your t's.

Matthew 5: 17-20

This particular passage speaks to a very critical and crucial dilemma that we now face and struggle with. The struggle that we speak of is that of trying to do what we desire and not strive to maintain the statues of the entire Bible. In this scripture, it says that not one jot or tittle shall pass; till it is all fulfilled. Now consider this beloved; a jot and tittle is the dot over the I and the cross in the t, and this is teaching there is a small difference in the two so they may seem similar in nature but different in their input; because in our translation it is our c and e and as you can tell the only difference in these two letters is a stroke of the pen at the top of the c. Many times in life we feel as if doing good will constitute for the other things in life we are doing wrong; **NOT SO**! You see the Pharisees; which are spoken of in these verse thought that they could live good enough to inherit Heaven; this is not the case! The goal of Jesus was to come and tie the two dispensations of Law and Grace together. We were told as younger kids thou shalt not kill, thou shalt not steal, thou shalt not commit adultery, thou shalt have no other god before **ME** and what Jesus did when He **TIED** Grace into the Law it heightened the experience. Whereas He originally said: thou shalt not kill, He says now if you hate your brother; you are guilty of murder. When you harbor malice, roll your eyes in disgust and it makes you sick to your stomach at the sight of someone you have committed murder in the sight of God. Thou shalt not commit adultery; He says now: that if you look and lust or have a lingering liaison with someone who is appealing to your eyes; you have committed adultery! **WOW**, all that has happened is that He made the rules and regulations sterner to keep us from sin! My question to you concerning guidelines we are to follow is: Are your i's dotted and your t's crossed or have you satisfied with everything looking the same?

APPLICATION
FIFTY-ONE

Are You Feeling Faint?

Psalms 27:13

Felling faint is a terrible feeling. You seemingly cannot control your actions or movements and most times it is due to the fact that your equilibrium is off kilter! Sometimes it is because of what you have eaten or that your body is warning you that rest is needed! Either way the body is on automatic shut-down mode. Believe it or not; spiritually speaking your equilibrium can be off when you are not balanced with the necessity of your life and that is the Word of God, and as far as your intake. We try to make it on a spiritual snack and what we really need is a full course meal! Sometimes we are spiritually malnourished and it causes a feeling of uneasiness and pigheadedness. My question to you: Do you have a balanced diet?

APPLICATION
FIFTY-TWO

Come Down
So You Can Go Up

I Peter 5:6

Come down; so you can go up! Many times we pray and pray and pray and ask God to give us more, take us higher, and enlarge our territory. There are times we begin to question why it that our prayers are not answered is because we have not followed the prerequisites that have been laid before us. It is most disturbing and frustrating to struggle and strain to get all we can and can all we get but still do not seem to make any progress; then our issues becomes God is not coming to our rescue. The writer here in I Peter gives us the secret formula to go to the level we desire to go to and it is most simple; **COME DOWN; SO YOU CAN GO UP**, it is just that simple! He says humble; a word that introduces us to its polar opposite of pride! Sometimes we can never be blessed because we are so HIGH on our own horses. We have earned a degree. We have moved into a larger home. We now drive a luxury vehicle. We have a dime over a dollar and nobody can tell us **ANYTHING! COME DOWN**. God wants to share with us His plan by sending a word through someone you would not even hang with, and you look down on them; **COME DOWN**. There are instances whereas a Word is sent on Sunday mornings and instead of receiving the deposit God has for **YOU**, you cancel the transaction because it calls for you to **COME DOWN**. Coming down consists of deflating yourself of self that God might place the necessary things in you to cause an elevational element in you to take you to places you never could imagine! He says that we need to **HUMBLE** ourselves **UNDER** the mighty **HAND** of God; otherwise COME DOWN under HIS hand which will ultimately **LIFT, ELEVATE** and **EXALT** us in **DUE** time! Due times actually means: your **SEASON**. My question to you: **ARE YOU TRYING TO FORCE YOUR SEASON?**

To contact the Author:

Pastor M.E. Lyons
Email: melmanministries@gmail.com
Mobile: (214) 641-8115
Pastor's Office: (936) 634-6060

Mailing Address:
Attention: Pastor M.E. Lyons
751 Kilgore Drive 5a
Henderson, Texas 75652

Goodwill Missionary Baptist Church
812 East Lufkin Avenue
Lufkin, Texas 75901

Other Book(s) Written/Published:
Fresh Air Volume One
The Mind: The Pulpit of GOD
The testimony of the sheep . . . according to
Psalms 23
Sermons and Illustrations by M.E.